DOGS SET II

Old English Sheepdogs

Stuart A. Kallen

ABDO & Daughters

visit us at
www.abdopub.com

Published by Abdo & Daughters, 4940 Viking Drive, Suite 622, Edina, Minnesota 55435.

Copyright © 1998 by Abdo Consulting Group, Inc., Pentagon Tower, P.O. Box 36036, Minneapolis, Minnesota 55435 USA. International copyrights reserved in all countries. No part of this book may be reproduced in any form without written permission from the publisher.

Printed in the United States.

Cover Photo credits: Peter Arnold, Inc.
Interior Photo credits: Peter Arnold, Inc.

Edited by Bob Italia

Library of Congress Cataloging-in-Publication Data

Old English sheepdogs / Stuart A. Kallen.
     p. cm. -- (Dogs. Set II)
     Includes index.
     Summary: Describes the physical characteristics and habits of these loyal working dogs and the care they require as a pet.
     ISBN 1-56239-575-0
     1. Old English sheepdog--Juvenile literature. [1. Old English sheepdog. 2. Dogs.] I. Title. II. Series: Kallen, Stuart A., 1955- Dogs. Set II.
     SF429.04K35 1998
     636.737--dc21   97-14830
                                         CIP
                                         AC

Contents

Dogs and Wolves–
Close Cousins

Dogs have been living with humans for more than 12,000 years. Today, millions of dogs live in the world. Over 400 **breeds** exist. And, believe it or not, all dogs are related to the wolf.

Some dogs—like tiny poodles or Great Danes—may look nothing like wolves. But under their skin, every dog shares many feelings and **traits** with wolves.

The dog family is called Canidae, from the Latin word *canis*, meaning "dog." The canid family has 37 **species**. They include foxes, jackals, wild dogs, and wolves.

Opposite page: These sheepdogs are two years old.

Old English Sheepdogs

The history of the Old English sheepdog goes back at least 200 years. The first known picture of one is in an English painting from 1771. The artist Gainsborough painted the Duke of Buccleuch who had his arms around an Old English sheepdog.

Before they were loved by Dukes and Princes, sheepdogs were working dogs. Hundreds of years ago, the English countryside was a wild place. Wolves, bears, and other meat-eaters preyed on sheep and other farm animals. A large, powerful dog was needed to protect the sheep from wild animals. And the dog needed a long, warm **coat** as protection from wind, rain, and snow. This is why the sheepdog was first bred.

In the early 1700s sheepdogs were used in England and Scotland to drive sheep and cattle into town

markets. There was a tax on sport dogs and pets. But there was no tax on working dogs. Farmers cut off the tails of their dogs when they were three or four days old. Then the dog would not be taxed. Because of this practice, the dogs were nicknamed "Bobtails."

By the mid-1800s, sheepdogs became popular as pets. They were popular in America as well. Today, the Old English sheepdog is one of the more popular dog **breeds** in the world.

Sheepdogs are popular pets.

What They're Like

Old English sheepdogs arc big, fluffy, gentle dogs. They love hugs and kisses. They're smart, friendly, and don't fight with other dogs. Although large in size, sheepdogs are graceful. They can move around a room without making much noise.

Sheepdogs are at home in the city or the country. As working dogs, they are one of the best. They retrieve, watch, herd, swim, hunt, and tend cattle and sheep.

An Old English sheepdog is gentle and friendly. But it has a loud, ringing bark that will scare away burglars.

Opposite page: Sheepdogs are big, fluffy, gentle dogs.

Coat and Color

The Old English sheepdog has a long, shaggy, thick **coat**. The undercoat is waterproof, allowing the dog to swim in cold weather. People wonder how the sheepdog can see with all that hair over its eyes. Sheepdogs see very well. The long hair protects working sheepdogs from dust, wind, and glaring sun.

The stray hairs from brushings can be put to use. Old English sheepdogs shed three to five pounds of hair a year. Some people weave that fur into wool for socks and sweaters!

Sheepdogs are gray, blue, and white with patches of color. Their eye color depends on the color of their fur. Very dark eyes are thought to be best by breeders. But some Old English sheepdogs have blue, gray, or ivory colored eyes.

Opposite page: Old English sheepdogs have very thick fur.

Size

Old English sheepdogs are large, strong, and agile creatures. They may be about 22 inches (56 cm) or taller. They may weigh from 80 to 110 pounds (36 to 50 kg). The body of the sheepdog is tight and muscular. Their necks are long and graceful and well **coated** with hair. The heads are large and square with lots of room for their big brains. Their nose is big, black, and square. The ears are medium-sized and hang flat to the side of the head.

Old English sheepdogs have long, straight legs, coated with thick fur. Their feet are small and round with thick, hard pads.

Some Old English sheepdogs are born without tails. Others have their tails cut off, or cropped, when they are a few days old. The stub should not be more than 2 inches (5 cm) on a full-grown dog.

Sheepdogs are large, strong, and agile.

Care

Sheepdogs make happy members of any family. They are gentle, relaxed, and loyal.

Like any dog, a sheepdog needs the same thing a human needs: a warm bed, food, water, exercise, and lots of love.

Some sheepdogs have hair that is easily matted, and needs to be brushed every day. Some do not. Other sheepdogs only need to be brushed once a week. Each owner has to decide how often to brush.

If the dog spends time outdoors, it will get dirty. Most of the dirt can be removed by brushing. It's hard to bathe a big, shaggy sheepdog. It should only be done once a month or the dog's fur will get matted. Puppies should not be bathed until they are six months old.

All dogs need shots every year. These shots stop diseases such as **distemper** and **hepatitis**.

As a member of your household, your dog expects love and attention. Sheepdogs enjoy human contact. They love to be taken for walks where they can run and explore.

A sheepdog getting a wash.

Feeding

Like all dogs, sheepdogs like to eat meat. But sheepdogs need a well-balanced diet. Most dog foods—dry or canned—will give the dog proper **nutrition**.

When you buy a puppy, find out what it has been eating and continue the diet. A small puppy needs four or five small meals a day. By six months, it will need only two meals a day. By one year, a single evening feeding will be enough.

Sheepdogs must be exercised every day so they do not gain weight. Walking, running, and playing together will keep you and your dog happy and healthy. Give your dog a hard rubber ball to play with.

Like any animal, sheepdogs need fresh water. Keep water next to the dog's food bowl and change it daily.

Sheepdogs need good food and exercise.

Things They Need

A dog needs a quiet place to sleep. A soft dog bed in a quiet corner is the best place for a sheepdog to sleep. A sheepdog should live indoors. If the dog must live outside, give it a dry, **insulated** dog house.

Sheepdogs love to play and explore. A fenced-in yard is the perfect home for the dog. If that is not possible, use a chain on a runner.

In most cities and towns, a dog must be leashed when going for a walk. It also needs a license. A dog license has the owner's name, address, and telephone number on it. If the dog runs away, the owner can be called.

Opposite page: Sheepdogs like to live indoors.

Puppies

A sheepdog can have up to eight puppies. The dog is **pregnant** for about nine weeks. When she is ready to give birth, she prefers a dark place away from noises. If your dog is pregnant, give her a strong box lined with an old blanket. She will have her puppies there.

Puppies are tiny and helpless when born. They arrive about a half hour apart. The mother licks them to get rid of the birth sacs and to help them start breathing. Their eyes are shut, making them blind for their first nine days. They are also deaf for about ten days.

After about four weeks, puppies begin to grow teeth. When this happens, separate them from their mother and give the puppies soft dog food.

A mother sheepdog with her puppies.

Glossary

breed: a grouping of animals with the same traits.

coat: the dog's outer covering of hair.

distemper: a contagious disease that dogs and other animals carry that is caused by a virus.

hepatitis (hep-uh-TIE-tis): an inflammation of the liver caused by a virus.

insulation (in-suh-LAY-shun): something that stops heat loss.

mammal: a group of animals, including humans, that have hair and feed their young milk.

nutrition (new-TRISH-un): food; nourishment.

pregnant: with one or more babies growing inside the body.

species (SPEE-sees): a kind or type.

trait: a feature of an animal.

veterinarian: a doctor trained to take care of animals.

Internet Sites

Old English Sheepdogs
http://152.160.144.200/houseofrex/
This site offers photos of various sheepdogs and also breed-ing information. It talks about how to care for your animal and where they come from.

The Official Old English Sheepdog Web Page
http://www.wwwins.net.au/dog/OES/menu.html
This site has many links to other sites. It also has a easy-to-use table of contents that includes history, grooming, train-ing, breeding, and much more.

Glencroft
http://infoweb.magi.com/~glncroft/
This site is really fun, it has sound and many links. Here you'll find lots of information on the Old English Sheepdog; Breed Characteristics, The Canadian OES Breed Standard, Grooming Help, Photographs: Show Photos & Snapshots, also information on The Old English Sheepdog & Owners' Club of Canada, and various "Doggie" Links - including a link to "The Official OES Web Page".

These sites are subject to change. Go to your favorite search engine and type in Old English Sheepdog for more sites.

Index